LIFE CENTRE

Copyright© 2001 by Barry Buzza

First published as a Life Pathways paperback 2001

All rights reserved. Printed in Canada

Unless otherwise indicated, Scripture quotations are from the

New American StandardBible,

© the Lockman Foundation 1960, 1962, 1963, 1968, 1971,

1972, 1973, 1975, 1977.

The text of this book is composed in FB Californian-Roman

Composition by TBA+D
Budget Printing
Book design by Jennifer Roberts

Library of Canadian Cataloguing in Publication Data
Buzza, Barry J. (Barry James), 1947 -
1. Self-realization --Religious aspects. 2. Spiritual life.
II. Title.
BL624.B889 2001
291.4'4   C00-911391-6

ISBN 0-9687652-1-1

Life Pathways
1460 Lansdowne Drive, Coquitlam, BC, Canada V3E 2N9

LIFE CENTRE

A PRIMER ON SPIRITUAL ALIGNMENT

BARRY JAMES BUZZA

LIFE
PATHWAYS

This book is dedicated to
my dad and mom,
who not only taught me how to respond to God's invitation,
but who also showed me how to live a spiritually centred life.

PART III How Do You Get There From Here?

Choose yourself today whom you will serve... but as for me and my family, we will serve the Lord.

CONTENTS

I wasn't really eavesdropping. Actually, I was trying to ignore the conversations around me that day by the pool so I could finish reading my book - but the young couple were so intense in their discussion that I couldn't help but listen. She was reading to her young husband excerpts from a psychology text and he was expounding his views on the subject.

After reading a section on the human soul she asked him what his thoughts were. I don't think he had a clue what he was saying, but in an effort to impress her, he shared his opinions freely. "Well, your soul is the part inside of you that feels and thinks and wonders," he said. (Doing okay so far.) "But we all have this other part to us. You could call it your spiritual centre. Some people go to church, others do yoga and some people shave their heads to get in touch with their spiritual centre."

As quickly as her husband said the words spiritual centre she laughed and responded, "Oh yeah, you mean our confused part!"

"That's exactly what I was thinking, he shot back. "Actually I don't think anybody has the goods on that mystery!"

In the midst of their conversation I became lost in my own thoughts. If I had been sitting a little closer to that couple and had had the opportunity, I would have loved to have got in on their discussion. I wondered how I would explain to someone who had no Christian background about what our Creator says about our spiritual centre. What lights could I turn on that would help bring clarity to such a mysterious dimension of our humanness?

We all wonder about the spiritual side of our make-up. We all ask questions about the deep unknowns of life:

Where did I come from?

Is there a God?

Does he know me or care about me?

Do I have a purpose?

Is there meaning to my life?

If there is a God, can I know him?

Where will I go when I die?

The young lady I overheard talking that day was serious in her questioning. She really wanted to know the answers. Something or someone was motivating her to seek understanding of the hidden areas of her soul.

I flipped open the small notebook that I always keep handy and quickly wrote down a few thoughts which came to my mind. Each of them sheds a slightly different coloured light on the subject of the couple's discussion. Each in its own way illustrates the answer to the most basic of our ominous questions - How can I find spiritual meaning to my existence?

As you read the thoughts that I penned that day by the pool, examine each of the pictures and see if you can spot the common thread joining my stories. Perhaps God will use one of them, or all of them, to give you insight into the mystery of your spiritual centre and how it relates to every other facet of your life journey.

Try imagining that the God who created you is shining his spotlight on the path ahead of you as you begin your sincere search for answers. Then whisper a simple prayer like this: *God please help me as I begin this adventuresome and somewhat mystical journey. Please light the way and guide my footsteps down the right path. Show me where to look and direct my thoughts as I read. Thank you.*

PART I

What Does it Mean to Be Connected?

Seek first his kingdom and his righteousness,
and all these things will be added unto you.

CHAPTER ONE

The Wheel and It's Axle

There is an interconnectedness intended
Many years ago when our daughters were young,
Kelly, the eldest, was ready to move up from her first
tiny two-wheeler to a girl's ten-speed bike. We gave
her the shiny new bicycle for Christmas in 1979. Her
old one, which had been used with training wheels for
each of our children, was ready to be discarded - it
had served its purpose. As I was placing the small
bike at the curb for spring cleanup a few months after
Christmas, the thought occurred to me that our lives
could be well illustrated by those bicycle wheels.

I unbolted the two wheels and threw the frame of
the bike away. Then I took a hefty pair of wire cutters

and removed the axle from the centre of one of them. The two wheels, one with an axle in place and the other without, have served me many times since that day as pictures of two lives - one life with its spiritual centre in place and the other life with its spiritual centre missing. The wheel rim to me was a clear picture of the intended purpose of every life. The tire and rim were created to roll down the road with the purpose of getting a rider from one place to another. The Triumph or CCM Company each had destiny in mind when they manufactured their bicycle wheels.

Our lives also were created for a purpose, with destiny in mind. Much more important than a bicycle, each of us is designed by the eternal engineer, our creator God, to accomplish a very meaningful purpose.

As I looked at the whole wheel, I also noticed that each of its spokes was necessary to help the wheel rim and tire fulfill their purpose. They connected the rim securely to its axle. The axle held each of the spokes in place giving strength to the wheel, and the spokes in turn kept the axle centred in the bicycle wheel.

In my imagination, the spokes of the wheels from my daughter's bike represented the many facets of

Bicycle Wheel With Axle

Ready to use for its
intended purpose.

Bicycle Wheel With No Axle

LOOSE SPOKES

The spokes are
not connected, so the
wheel is useless.

our lives which give life meaning. Our work, leisure,
marriage, family, schooling, sleep, friendship, sexuali-
ty, money, energy and time are each depicted by a
different spoke. In its own way each dimension of
our lives brings fulfillment, pleasure and meaning to
our existence. But clearly, unless each of the spokes
is connected to its centre, which is represented by
the axle, it will never fulfill the distinct responsibili-
ty for which it was made.

No axle; no use

The key part of the bicycle wheel is its axle. Around
it everything else revolves. When the axle is in its

rightful place, the bicycle wheel can fulfill its destined purpose. The axle represents the very core of our person. The wise King Solomon, who reigned in Israel's finest hour three thousand years ago, said it this way; *He has made everything appropriate in its time. He has also set eternity in our hearts.* The eternity that God has set in the core of our being is our spiritual centre or our God part. The axle when properly placed is the very heart of all that we are and were ever intended to be. If it isn't in place, our lives will be ultimately meaningless. However, when it is in place, every other dimension of our lives (the spokes) can be connected to our spiritual centre (the axle) and we will be prepared to fulfill our God assigned purpose.

That's the reason that I keep those two little bicycle wheels in my office closet. Time after time, as I've sat with people who are looking for the mystical something missing in their lives, I bring out my daughter's bicycle wheels. It's fun to watch the lights go on when sincere seekers finally understand what the missing element is in their lives! They discover that they were created with an eternal spiritual dimension.

The italicized words that I introduced this first

part with are the words of Jesus to all who are looking to make sense of their lives; *Seek first the Kingdom of God* (the axle) *and his righteousness,* (this word simply means his right order, which is symbolized by all the spokes secured to the axle) *and all these things* (safety, security, significance, identity, love, purpose, destiny, which are represented by the rim and tire) *will be added unto you.*

The first picture I drew by the pool that day answers the question - how can I find spiritual meaning to my life? I find it by understanding that I was created with a spiritual dimension, which must be securely centred in all that I am and in all that I do.

I trust that this sheds some light on your path as you search for meaning and power to your life. I still have not answered the questions: How do I get my centre (the axle) in place? or How can I connect up the different dimensions (the spokes) of my life to the centre? But read on! I'll turn on another switch and see if it helps clear up a little more of the mystery.

CHAPTER TWO

A Bountiful Garden

The apple tree and its branches ‑ there is a life flow intended

Abide in me, and I in you. As the branch cannot bear fruit of itself unless it abides in the vine, so neither can you unless you abide in me. I am the vine, you are the branches; he who abides in me and I in him, he bears much fruit, for apart from me you can do nothing.

Last fall a friend of mine gave me a wonderful gift. This spring I threw it away. I felt very bad about the loss, but the gift was thoroughly dead by the time spring came and therefore served virtually no purpose.

The gift that he gave to me was several branches from his prolific raspberry patch. I had admired his plants last summer and so, in his kindness, when the growing season was over, he cut some sprigs for me. The problem was not with the raspberry plants, but rather that I had neglected to put them in the ground where they could have been nurtured. I forgot all about the cuttings through the winter season and then by the time spring arrived when I discovered my neglect, it was too late. The branches were dead and they could no longer produce raspberries. What a great loss! The raspberry branches were disconnected from their life source, which would have promoted their life and any fruit that they could have produced.

Lessons from our gardens

It was my father who first sparked my interest in gardening. I'm certainly no expert, but I do love to see new life spring forth every year. It never ceases to amaze me as I watch an apple tree that appeared to be dead throughout the winter, come to life in March and April. First the leaves, then the blossoms and finally the apples appear. Every year it's the same - leaves, blossoms and apples. In that seasonal cycle, there are many lessons about our spiritual nurture, growth, fruitfulness and reproduction.

One of the unforgettable lessons that my dad taught me years ago was how to graft a branch into a tree. I've seen him fill in bare spots on an ornamental tree trunk by adding branches from other trees. I've watched with awe as he grafted different coloured leafed branches on one tree so that in the spring it would bear multicoloured blossoms, as well as a variety of shaped leaves. He has also grafted two or three types of apples into one trunk so that the tree was not only more fruitful, but so that it would also produce different tasting apples all at the same time.

The way my dad taught me to graft was to carefully slice into the main branch at just the right time, opening it up to its living core; then to place the new branch into the cut area so that the heart of the small branch could connect to the heart of the main stem; finally to cover the joint in pitch and wrap it carefully in string.

He explained to me that God does the rest of the miracle by joining the two entities into one. Eventually the branch that has been grafted in lives and grows as an integral part of the large established tree. The two literally become one tree. The new

branch, with the life flowing through the root sys-
tem of the tree, up the trunk and through the spliced
joint, produces leaves, blossoms and fruit. They are
thoroughly connected, just as if the grafted branch
had been part of the tree since its beginning.

We are the branches

Look again at the verse that I introduced this section
with; *I* (Jesus) *am the vine, you* (that's whoever is grafted into the main vine) *are the branches; he who abides in
me and I in him, he bears much fruit, for apart from me you can
do nothing.* The idea conveyed in this verse is that we
are disconnected right from birth. Just like those
raspberry branches that I threw away the following
spring, if we are not grafted into the life flow of the
main vine on time, we will not only be fruitless (that

is we will not fulfill our life purpose), but we will eventually die.

We all need the master gardener to skillfully cut the main vine. When he does this, he lovingly places us in relationship to him so that his spiritual life flows through our spirit, soul and body; we then become secure, nourished, cared for and purposeful!

We'll see later how God sent his son Jesus, to die on a Roman cross (he was severely cut), so that we could be grafted into his spiritual life flow. When that connection happens, we find our place in his orchard and begin the cyclical process of producing life that is inherently reproducible for generations to come. The amazing conclusion to this metaphor is that every apple that grows from our branches has seeds within it, which could eventually reproduce countless crops of apples. The influence of a healthy life continues for generations beyond us.

In the bicycle and axle metaphor, we saw how each of us must find our spiritual centre and insure that every facet of our lives is securely connected so that we can fulfill our purpose. Then we've seen in the apple tree and branches metaphor how each of us, as disconnected branches, needs to be vitally grafted to the living tree which is securely anchored to the ground, so that there is life flowing through us and we can grow the fruit that we were designed to produce.

You might have noticed from this story about grafting that we need external help to become what we were created to be. The apple tree needs both a creator and a skilful gardener. The principle that I'm underlining in this second picture is called transcendence. We all need something or someone outside of ourselves to help us find our identity and fulfill our purpose. That external help must come from God. He's the loving and capable creator and gardener who makes the spiritual connection possible.

CHAPTER THREE

The Joy of Marriage

The wedding - there is a choice involved
For this reason a man shall leave his father and mother and shall be joined to his wife, and the two shall become one flesh. This mystery is great; but I am speaking with reference to Christ and the church.

Although it took place almost forty years ago, I can remember the day as if it were yesterday. My brother and I were leaving on a three month trip by ship and motorcycle across the Atlantic and Europe, but first we had to cross Canada by train. A few of our friends came to see us off on that mild April evening. Among them was a very beautiful young woman who tagged along with a mutual friend. Her name was Susan. After a short visit, Dave and I left the Vancouver station and said good-bye to our friends. As I took one more awkward glance at Susan before the last call came, our eyes met. There was destiny in that quick visual exchange.

The Wedding

Almost six months later, I saw her again. I was seated on the front row of our church and Susan, her sister and our mutual friend were singing up front. There was something about her smile and the way that her eyes lit up that captured my rapt attention. Still too shy to connect with her and Susan just having turned fifteen, I let her slip away once more.

Two months later on my birthday, our mutual friend Linda, invited me over after night classes, to the house where she was boarding. We were going to order in Chinese food. When I arrived, Linda greeted me at the door. As I glanced over her shoulder, there was Susan. This was her family's home!

I turned twenty that night and somehow managed to get a birthday kiss as a present. I was in love! That kiss was placed on my lips over forty years ago, and I can still feel it today! There was destiny in our kiss. I don't think there has been a total of thirty nights that I have not kissed that young lady since February 22, 1967! We were engaged on Valentine's Day the next year and married on February 28, 1969.

Marriage pictures a covenantal relationship

I've given you a summary of our happy story because it illustrates another facet of the relationship that God desires to have with each of us. If you are able, think of him as being the groom and us the bride. (I know that's a difficult picture for us guys to see, but it's an accurate metaphor of our spiritual bond. The fact is that the concept of marriage originated with God as an illustration of the covenantal nature of his love for us.)

Here's how it works. There are three phases to the process. First, the emotionally charged days of falling in love; second, the act of getting married; and third, both the challenging and joyful years of being married.

Understanding that marriage is an ongoing process is helpful. With Susan and me, the falling in love emotionally did not take very long. That was the easy part; but then followed two years of getting to know each other before we were ready to say our wedding vows. People don't usually fall in love and get married on the same day. It takes time for our minds and wills to catch up with our emotions. Even since our wedding day over thirty-seven years ago, we have continued the process of coming to fully understand one another.

In terms of our being married to God, although he has known us from conception, we still need to get to know him, learn to trust him and come to love him before we are ready to fully commit our life to his care. The simple diagram on the following page might help us to get a bird's eye view of the entire process.

Phase I - Falling in love

The first couple of steps are the falling in love phase. Before the marriage vows there are physical attraction,

The Maturing Marriage Relationship

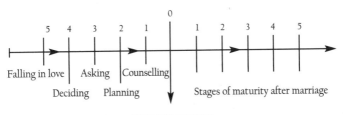

THE WEDDING

emotional attachment, intellectual interaction and willful actions involved. In our relationship to God, there is also the involvement of our emotions, intellect and wills, but there is also another whole new dimension. As we start growing in our relationship with God, the deep empty spiritual vacuum inside of us begins to be filled.

We could compare the spiritual vacuum, on a superficial level, with putting together a jigsaw puzzle. You've completed the sky, forest and lakeside and the picture is looking almost exactly like the one printed on the box cover, but there's a piece missing. Search as you may you cannot find the missing piece, and in your frustration you are ready to throw the entire incomplete picture away; but wait...you discover a piece of the puzzle sticking out from under the tossed box. Does it fit? Your heart is pounding as you pick up the last piece of the jigsaw puzzle and put it into place. A perfect match! Now doesn't that sense of accomplishment feel wonderful!

Placing that missing piece is a very limited illustration, but it is a picture of the growing realization that Jesus Christ is the missing piece of the puzzle that we've been looking for all of our life. He is the only one who can fill the spiritual emptiness inside us, and complete the picture of our life.

The falling in love phase is the process of discovery. In pre-marriage, we spend hundreds of hours, sometimes happily and other times in deep frustration, discovering more and more about this person whom we are planning to marry. It's the same with our relationship to God. Before giving the controls of our life to him, it makes just as much sense to learn as much as possible about who this Power is, with whom we are considering establishing an eternal relationship.

The premarital phase before the wedding continues with a few more stopping places. There's the deciding, asking, positive response, planning the wedding ceremony and preparing yourselves with positive counsel. All are necessary parts of the journey. Finally, at the wedding, in addition to the decorations, fancy dress, order of service, pictures, reception, food and dancing, there are two indispensable acts - the vow and the legal contract. We'll come to them in a moment.

So you've decided to pop the question. You know that there are going to be difficult sections along the road ahead, but you've considered the costs and have made the decision. Working up the courage you ask, "Will you marry me? I'd love to spend the rest of my life as your husband." She of course jumps up and down (you hope) screaming, "Yes, yes, yes!"

Then comes the planning and the paying for the wedding. During that preparatory stage you and your fiancee spend several weeks in premarital classes, talking, laughing, crying and getting ready for the big day.

The pre-Christian process

In the same way, most people who hear about God for the first time, don't instantly fall in love with him and decide to spend the rest of their life serving him. There is also a falling in love phase in our relationship with God. Some of us are initially drawn to him because of a sense of spiritual need, while others are drawn by an emotional or intellectual need. We are each wired differently.

A person who is more cognitive might be studying the awesome mysteries of DNA and come to realize that human life was obviously not an accidental happening. He may be watching a program on the *Discovery* channel about the wonders of our galaxies or be reading a biography of a great leader whose life was changed when he encountered Christ. Maybe she has a good friend who is a believer and having watched the way that friend handled stress, wishes she could have that same inner peace. It may be an age factor; the person has just turned thirty or forty, got married or had her first child, and becomes aware of a missing element in her inner spiritual life.

Very often, as it is when we meet someone to whom we feel drawn, there is an initial emotional attraction. With a person's coming to God, he may be sitting in the funeral service of his mother and wonder for the first time what happens to us when we die. Or just as likely, it may not be the death of a person, but the death of a marriage or the loss of his job that first brings that person to his sense of need. The valleys of life press us into emotional openness. Inner tension because of relational conflict, lack of money, ill health, or job stress can all be factors in the feelings which attract a person to the peace and fulfillment which God offers.

Then again, others are drawn to God because they are honestly facing the deep spiritual needs of life. We all have an inborn belief in God, a sense of right and wrong, feelings of guilt because of poor choices that we have made and an abiding sense of loneliness until that spiritual vacuum inside of us is filled with God.

Regardless of whether it is our intellectual curiosity, emotional needs or spiritual emptiness that redirect us to pursue a relationship with God, you can understand that this falling in love phase is a process. That process may take a few days or in some cases, several years before leading us to the altar of decision.

Phase II - The marriage ceremony

Finally the wedding day arrives. Bride and groom, your bridesmaids and groomsmen, as well as your family and friends are ready for the critical second phase - the marriage ceremony. Now comes the two most important parts of this wedding. They are the vow that you are making before God, family and friends to each other, pledging to love, honor and be faithful; and the legal contract which you both, your attendants and the pastor must sign. When you have said the vows, which are the heart of the marriage, and have signed the document, making it a legal agreement, you have completed phase two.

Just as it is an intense, exhilarating and challenging road that leads to the day of the wedding, so it is with the spiritual journey that you have already embarked on. You have discovered that there is another whole dimension to life - the spiritual world. You likely have many questions: Is Jesus the only way to God? What happens to me if I don't give my life to God? Does he really care one way or the other? What about Church? Isn't it full of hypocrites? How can I know that Jesus really is God? Can I trust the Bible? What am I getting myself into?

Every journey begins with just one step. Trust that voice inside you. Take one step forward. Test it out. You'll know instinctively if you are headed down the right path or not. My point is simply that your spiritual journey is one of daily discovery. Enjoy each day of your unfolding relationship with God just as you might enjoy a growing romance with your future life partner.

The Bible says; *As many as received him, to them he gave the right to become children of God, even to those who believe in his name.* In that statement is written three of the steps in our marriage to God: believe, receive and become.

My *believing* that Susan would make an awesome wife, my loving her and wanting to live with her for the rest of my life were not enough. I had to *receive* her as my wife on that clear, crisp Friday evening of 1969, by vowing to love her and by signing the legal agreement. Only then were we ready for the third and final ongoing phase - marriage.

Phase III - The joyful years of being married

For Susan and me, it took the first couple of years of marriage to really understand our own responsibilities and privileges in our new relationship. She had to give a little and I had to give a little. We bumped into each other's habits and expectations many times as we were making the adjustments that were needed. By about the third year, we began moving in harmony with each other, but the process continues. Thirty years later, I'm still learning how Susan thinks, and she is still trying to understand my motives, moods and attitudes.

Marriage for all of us is a work in progress, but the trade-off is well worth the effort. The love, friendship and happiness, added to memories together, children and grandchildren, and hopes for the future are the rewards that we enjoy as a result of planting and nurturing positive seeds early in the relationship.

Jesus calls phase three *becoming*. Becoming is the third step after believing and receiving. After receiving Jesus as your personal saviour by making a commitment such as follows, you begin the life-long process of becoming like him.

Here's a simple prayer, we'll come back to later, that you could consider praying as a commitment to God:

Father God, I humbly acknowledge that I have sinned and that I am a sinner. I am guilty of deliberate wrongdoing and my sins have separated me from your holy presence. I am helpless in restoring our broken relationship.

I firmly believe that Jesus is your son and that he died on the cross for my sins and suffered in my place, taking the punishment I deserved.

I have thoughtfully counted the cost of following you. I sincerely turn away from my past sins. I willingly surrender to you as my Lord and Master.

I now receive your son, Jesus, as my Saviour. I believe that he has patiently been waiting outside the door of my life knocking. I now open the door. Come in Lord Jesus, and be my Saviour and Friend forever. Amen.

The crossroad

There's one more thing about the marriage ceremony. Remember the ring? After you and your spouse said, "I do," you placed a ring on each other's finger, which serves as a permanent seal of the agreement that you've made. As I look at my thirty-seven year old gold wedding ring, I am reminded of the vow, which I am bound to, that I made with my wife before God.

In the spiritual vow that you and God are making, God promises that he will give you his Holy Spirit to live inside of you as a seal of your mutual agreement. Here is how he says it; *In him, you also, after listening to the message of truth, the gospel of your salvation - having also believed, you were sealed in him with the Holy Spirit of promise.*

When you pray to God and ask Jesus to forgive your sins and have the ultimate authority in your life, several miracles happen in an instant of time: you are totally forgiven of all your sins, past, present and future; you receive gifts of his faith, hope and love; you are guaranteed an eternal home in heaven; and God's invisible presence, whom he calls the Holy Spirit, comes inside of you. He is there as a seal to remind you of your relationship with God (that's like your wedding ring, which serves as a reminder of your marriage vow); he helps you understand the purpose of your life and how to make wise choices; and he empowers you to live your life according to his plan.

It's our choice

At the heart of both your marriage to your spouse and your relationship to God, there is a choice. God made his choice even before he created the world. You were his choice - he has had his eye on you since before you were a twinkle in your father's eye. Now you are at an important crossroad of life - you need to make a choice. Do you choose Jesus? Do you want to spend the rest of your life in a loving relationship with him?

I've walked down this pathway with enough people to understand how challenging this crossroad decision is. Any change comes with resistance. This exchange that occurs at the very core of our life is a huge step. You are making a decision to remove yourself from the control room of your life and allow God to take your place. You are agreeing to follow his plans and directions from now on.

At one level of your consciousness, you may be feeling, "Wow, am I giving up my freedom to do my own thing? What about my hopes, plans and dreams? Can I really be happy doing what God has planned for me?

Then at a deeper spiritual level, you may be thinking, "This is what I've been looking for all my life. Of course, it's the best way! God made me and so he knows what's the right path for me to walk."

Perhaps you're feeling, like many do, a deep sense of spiritual excitement. Finally, that emptiness that you've been trying to fill for years is going to be satisfied. Keep reading! It gets even better in the next chapter. We'll be talking about understanding our identity, our purpose and discovering a new life dynamic that you may have only dreamed about!

PART II

There's a Powerflow Intended

*This gospel is the power of God for salvation
to everyone who believes.*

CHAPTER FOUR

This Little Light of Mine

I don't know a better way to explain what I am about to write to you, than to describe it as an "Aha!" moment. I'm sure you've had them before - maybe when you realized that meeting a certain person was not a coincidence but a God-incident; you got an inspiration for a new way of doing something; a disappointing experience, such as getting fired from your job, suddenly took a turn and you realized that it was the best thing that could have happened to you; or you finally discovered that lost piece to the puzzle and it all came together! That's what I call an "Aha!" moment.

My prayer is that these next few pages will turn

37

on a light inside you; that you will understand how important you have always been to God, how much he loves you and how he wants to see you spiritually alive and thoroughly fulfilled! May this become an "Aha!" moment in your life journey.

The power of electricity

In our kitchen we have several appliances - a stove, fridge, blender, toaster, can opener, coffee grinder and other such conveniences. Although each of them is very different in purpose and function, they all have something in common. You know what it is - electricity.

Is a toaster a toaster when it is not plugged into electricity? Is a fridge still a fridge when it has no power? I guess technically they are in name, but the toaster or the fridge will never fulfill the purpose for

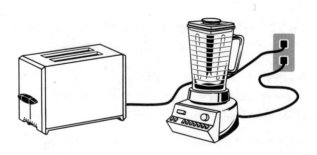

which it was created until it is plugged into its power source and turned on. Appliances are rather common and unholy in comparison to people, but they do provide an interesting picture of the external power that is necessary for us to fulfill our personal purpose.

Our kitchen appliances all have intrinsic value, identity and purpose. Our toaster for example is a beauty. I paid about eighty dollars for it, so it has value. It is a General Electric toaster-oven, so it has identity. It was created to serve as both a toaster and an oven, so it has a clear purpose. But none of its value, identity or purpose has any meaning unless it is attached by plug to an active power source.

That by the way is another whole story. The toaster may be plugged into a kitchen electrical outlet, but if there is no power in the house or if it is not wired up to the power source properly, even when it is plugged in, it won't give the toaster meaning because it still is not fulfilling its purpose. Likewise we can be plugged into an external source such as science, wealth, business, success, family or fame, but there will still be no transcendent eternal power flow. Everything short of being plugged into the creator, the sustainer of the universe, will fall short of empowering us to fulfill all that we were created to be!

Transcendence, identity and community

So that you don't get lost in my kitchen scenario, what does all of this mean to your search to spiritual meaning in your life? Every person has three essential needs which must be met in order to find fulfillment. Our needs are for *transcendence*, which is being securely anchored beyond ourself to something or someone bigger and stronger than we are (like a boat in a storm being anchored to a large rock); *identity*, which is finding meaning and purpose in our life, knowing who we are, where we came from, why we are here and where we are headed both now and after death; and *community*, which is finding love, acceptance and forgiveness. Community is knowing that we belong somewhere, that somebody loves us and that we love others.

The appliance picture, like the branch and vine, illustrates our need for transcendence. The appliance must be plugged into the power source and the branch must be attached to the main vine for each to fulfill what their creators intended. But our kitchen appliances also have another story to tell. They do not really see their identity fulfilled until the power source is turned on. Only when they are properly hooked up to the power, can the toaster begin to toast bread, the fridge cool milk, the can opener open cans and the coffee grinder grind coffee beans. Identity and fulfillment are only a hope and dream until the power is turned on and begins to flow through us.

My four electric light bulbs

Do you see the relationship to your own life? Do you see the possibility of your personal purpose and identity coming to life when you are plugged into God, the ultimate power source?

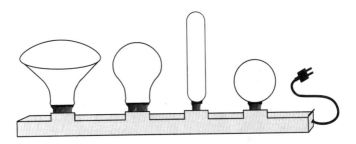

I have in my office a power bar with four light sockets in it and a plug. In the four sockets, I've placed four very different light bulbs - a red spot-light, a yellow bug light, a green tube light and a small white refrigerator-light. I use this contraption to teach people about identity.

There are some things that all four of my bulbs have in common. They each have a glass casing, a fil-ament inside and a screw shaped base on the bot-tom, but as much as they are similar in some respects, each serves a very different purpose. The red spotlight is used to light up our garden outside every Christmas. The yellow bulb is for outside on our porch so that bugs will not be attracted to our sitting area. The green bulb is to decoratively light behind a display case, and the small light is for the inside of our refrigerator.

Their worth and identity are intrinsic in their unique personal purposes. When the power is turned on, they figuratively come into their own. They come alive! If there were no power, they may look worth-while on their exterior, but they would never really be fulfilled. However, when the electricity flows, they become all that they were created to be.

Some people are afraid that they will lose their identity if they become a Christian (the word

Christian simply means a follower of Jesus Christ), but the opposite is actually true. That one hundred watt yellow bug light is a one hundred watt yellow bug light regardless of its being plugged in or not. It looks the same both ways, but when it is hooked up to the power source it begins to fulfill its destiny. It becomes worthwhile. The power does not change it into a spotlight or a night-light, rather it enables it to become the bug light that it was created to be!

Likewise, when you are plugged into God through Jesus Christ you will become the person who God created you to be! You will be purposeful and fulfilled. King Solomon said; *The spirit of a man is the lamp of the Lord*. Jesus said; *We are the light of the world*. Both statements become true only when we are plugged into God.

CHAPTER FIVE

Sons, Stones, Deposits and Butterflies

Here are a few more word pictures from the Bible to help more clearly illuminate the spiritual meaning of your life:

Adoption

When we adopt a son or daughter, they become fully ours. We love and honor our adopted child just as much as our own flesh and blood. God, as a loving parent, chooses to adopt us into his royal family, giving us all the full rights of sonship, even to the point of putting our names in his will.

Stones in a temple

Just as a stone mason skillfully crafts rough stones
so that he can construct a stone wall or building,
each of us is symbolically a stone in the temple of
God. The temple will not be completed until every
stone is in place. The stone mason (God) is cutting
and shaping the stones (us) in the quarry of life
every day for use in his temple.

A deposit put into your account

Each of us will one day have to stand before God for
a final accounting of how worthwhile or worthless
our life has been. The fact is that all of us fall short of
his requirements. We are all sinners - period!
Anything short of perfection is out of God's range of
acceptability.

Accountants would appreciate the biblical picture of being caught short on audit day. We have not
enough rightness in our spiritual accounts to pay the
debt we owe for our sin, so when we ask him to, God
deposits in our account his son Jesus' rightness.
When Jesus paid the debt for our sin with his life,
our account was topped up! When Jesus said, "It is
finished!" as his last words on the cross, he literally

meant that our spiritual debt was paid in full! I love that picture!

A Caterpillar becomes a butterfly

Another favorite word picture of mine is the process of metamorphosis. God uses the word metamorphosis to describe the change that happens to those who choose to follow God's way. We become sons and daughters of God. The mystical process is like a caterpillar becoming a butterfly. When the right time comes, the caterpillar grabs onto the underneath of a milkweed plant leaf with a specially designed pair of hooks on his hind legs and he hangs there upside down. Amazingly, a few days later a hard lump inside the larvae begins to swell and suddenly bursts the caterpillar's skin. This pupa pulls itself completely out of the caterpillar's skin and reaches up to grab onto the hardened silk with which the caterpillar

Caterpillar Becomes A Butterfly (Metamorphosis)

was fastened to the plant. The sun then hardens the bluish green shell called a chrysalis.

In about ten days another creature altogether, the Monarch butterfly, pushes her way out of the chrysalis. This process is called *metamorphosis*. It is a brand new creation which comes out of the old one as it dies. Although the butterfly comes out of the caterpillar, it is a new creation. The caterpillar had a mouth to chew its food, but the butterfly only drinks nectar through its proboscis. The caterpillar had six small eyes on each side of its head, two short antennae and eight pairs of legs. The butterfly has two compound eyes, two long antennae, only three pairs of legs and two wings.

When Mother Butterfly laid her eggs there were two sets of genetic information in them. One was the caterpillar and the other was the butterfly - one came out of the other. The caterpillar was metamorphosized. That's the word used in the Bible to describe the transformation process that happens to a person who receives God's gift of spiritual life - new life comes out of the old life. Our bodies remain the same, as do our temperament, personality, emotions and intellect, but a transformation takes place at our very core which vitalizes our conscience, motives and attitudes. We become spiritually awakened. The change that takes place in a person's life when he receives Jesus' free gift of forgiveness and eternal life is a mystery.

Trying to explain to an uninitiated person what a peach tastes like, what a worm feels like, what a cactus looks like, or what holding your baby for the first time is like, is difficult because words fall short! In order to be fully understood, each must be experienced. That's the way it is with our becoming a Christian; it's almost inexplicable unless we are transformed ourselves. Each of the pictures that I've described to you is only an incomplete glimpse of the wonder of enjoying peace with God. Only when you experience his love and forgiveness first hand will you fully understand. It will be one of those unforgettable "Aha!" moments.

PART III

How Do You Get There From Here?

Choose yourself today whom you will serve...
but as for me and my family, we will serve the Lord.

CHAPTER SIX

The Road to Somewhere

Frank Sinatra made the song, *My Way*, famous. He crooned with pride, "*I did it my way!*" and that was his rightful choice. Every person has a free will and can follow the life path that he chooses for himself. Freedom of choice is a priceless gift which God has given to all of us. I can choose to walk my way or his way. It's up to me.

For example, no one can make me learn basic arithmetic or history in school. I can choose to study and learn, or I can choose to play around while others are learning. It's my right to choose. The problem comes when I get to the end of the school year and I have to write the exam. Those who chose to learn will pass, while those who chose not to learn will fail. There will always ultimately be consequences to our choices. Perhaps I won't be able to continue my education because I haven't learned the basics; maybe I won't be able to get the job that I want or I won't be able to function as well as others in society. I can choose the way that I want to go on the path of life, but I must remember that there will be consequences to every choice that I make!

The path of life

In the Bible, God describes the path of life as the narrow, winding road that leads to what he calls abundant life. The pathway is not an easy one, but following it does promise the very things in life which we are all seeking - fulfillment, love, inner peace, security, identity, eternal life, strength to face difficulties and a relationship with God.

As for the streets in our neighborhood, we may choose to walk down a certain road to the store, or take another road. Sometimes in life there are two or three roads which will ultimately take us to the same place. But this is not so with the path of life. God's

Word tells us that there is only one way to go. Jesus said; *I am the way, the truth and the life. No one can come to the Father except through me.* One of the Old Testament writers, Joshua, put it this way; *Honour the Lord and serve him wholeheartedly...but if you are unwilling to serve the Lord, then choose today whom you will serve...but as for me and my family, we will serve the Lord.*

Think of your choice of life pathways like a fork in the road. Somewhere along your life journey, you will arrive at a crossroad. At that point (maybe it's before you right now) you have to carefully consider which road you will take for the rest of your life. One way is wide and easy, while the other is narrow and difficult. One way is where most people are going, while the other is chosen by only a few. One road leads to death, while the other leads to abundant life. Which one will you choose?

Deep down inside you will hear a voice telling you, "Take the path of life. It's the right way!"

Let's assume for a moment that you choose to take the path of life. You've counted the cost of the journey and now you are making a decision to follow God's way to abundant life. Take a look at this next diagram:

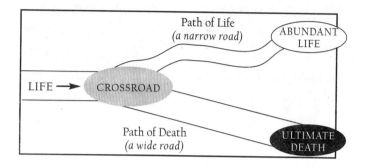

A huge chasm blocks the path

You've chosen to follow God's way and are feeling excited and happy about your choice, but as soon as you begin down the narrow road to fullness of life, you are confronted by a huge Grand Canyon - an impassable gulf between you and God. The chasm before you is your sin. God's way demands perfect obedience and we have all fallen short. Let's picture it like this:

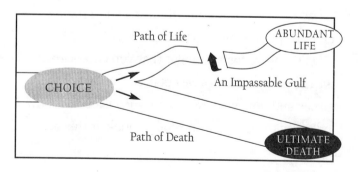

Imagine that the gulf, which separates you from God's promise of abundant life, is one hundred feet across and two hundred feet deep. There's no way that you can jump across it.

"But," you cry, "I'm a lot better than the guy down the street who beats his wife! I'm more honest than my co-worker. He cheats on his income tax! Surely I am good enough for God to accept me on the pathway of life!"

God responds, "Yes, you have lived better than your neighbour. If his behaviour were to determine the distance that he could jump, he'd only be able to jump ten feet across the chasm before he would fall to his death. Your co-worker has lived a little bit better than your neighbour, so he may be able to jump forty feet. But you, my son, have lived a good and victorious life - almost perfect. You could jump farther than most of your friends, maybe ninety-five feet, before you would fall to your death!"

Of course, all three of you would fail to cross the divide, you may be able to jump farther, but it would still not be far enough.

God's Word to us says that; *All have missed the mark; all fall short of God's glorious standard.* The fact is that none of us is perfect and we are all destined to fall short of the other side - to our death!

So what can we do? The answer to that question is a sad nothing. There is nothing that we can do. We cannot cross the impassable gulf on our own merit. Coming to God down the path of life is impossible in our own strength.

But there's good news!

There is good news - He's got a plan!

Before the world was even created, God was aware of this situation. He knew that we would continually choose our way over his way, that we would fall short of the requirements and that this gulf of sin would eternally separate us from him and the fullness of life that he wants us to enjoy. So before we were even born, he formulated a plan!

Because he knew that we could never get to him on our own, his plan was that he would come to us. Amazingly God, the creator of the universe, became a human being so that he could relate to you and me. He entered humanity, on what we celebrate as Christmas, as a baby born in Bethlehem about two thousand years ago. The name that God chose for the baby who was born was Jesus (which means Saviour). Jesus was the Christ (which means the Anointed One of God) born of the virgin Mary, and he came to bridge the gulf between us and God.

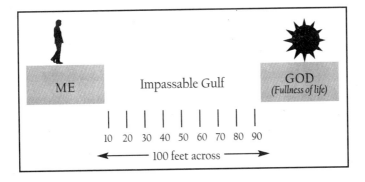

Although the story deserves much more explanation, the gist of it is that Jesus Christ lived a totally perfect, sinless human life. He was the only man who has ever done so and because of his perfection, he rightly deserved to cross the chasm along the path of life. He became the way to God and made it possible for us to come with him.

But there was still another problem. Even if we were to cross the gulf, our human sinfulness would prohibit us from coming into the presence of our perfect God. God would have had to be unjust to overlook our sin and simply accept us as we were. So unwilling to reject us, he allowed his son Jesus to represent all of mankind (men, women and children) and pay the debt that we owed for our sin. He says it this way; *For the wages of sin is death, but the free gift of God is eternal life through Jesus Christ our Lord.*

When Jesus died at the hands of Roman executioners on the cross almost two thousand years ago, he died in our place. His death paid the price of our sins, past, present and future. As I wrote earlier, the last three words which Jesus uttered on the cross were, "It is finished!" His words mean, *paid in full!* The debt of your sin has been covered! The possibility of your coming into relationship with God had now been secured. Here's a picture of how Jesus became the way to God:

Wow! That's what Jesus meant when he said; *I am*

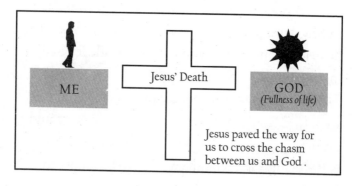

ME

Jesus' Death

GOD
(Fullness of life)

Jesus paved the way for us to cross the chasm between us and God .

the way, the truth and the life. No one can come to the Father except through me.

Do you remember the pictures that I began this book with? Let's see if we can tie the whole story together now.

The bicycle wheel

God wants to be at the very centre of every life. His intention is that every dimension of your life would be connected to him, the axle. That can only happen when you choose to walk across the bridge of God's forgiveness. Only when you get to the other side, by accepting Jesus' free gift of forgiveness and life, can God take his place at the spiritual centre of your life. The axle can finally become centred!

The apple tree and its branches

When you allow Jesus to be your bridge to God by accepting his payment of your debt of sin by his death on the cross, you are grafted into the true vine. Only then can his eternal life begin to flow through your spiritual veins; and only then can you produce the fruit you were designed to produce, which will have eternal value!

The wedding

Becoming a bride or a groom involves a choice - to believe and to receive. When you believe that Jesus Christ really is God in human form; that he was born of the virgin Mary and became a man, without ever sinning; and that he died in your and my place on the cross, you can then receive his gift of forgiveness and life. When you receive God's free gift, then he enables you to become his spiritual partner on the path of life.

The light bulb and electricity

As you cross the bridge that Jesus has provided, you are figuratively plugging into the power of God. That power, which enabled Jesus Christ to rise from the dead on Easter morning, now flows through your spiritual wires to enable you to become all that God purposed when he created you!

Sons, stones, deposits and butterflies

Receive God's gift of forgiveness and life and you are immediately adopted into his spiritual family; you become a stone skillfully quarried and shaped for use in his temple; he deposits sufficient rightness in your account to make you fully acceptable to our just God;

and you are metamorphosized, which means you become a brand new creation now walking down the path that leads to a purposeful and satisfying life.

Our basic human needs

I stated earlier that every believer has three primary needs which must be met before he can find meaning and fulfillment. Our three needs are: *transcendence*, which is the need to be connected to an anchor beyond ourselves; *identity*, which is the need to find meaning and purpose to our lives, to know where we came from, why we are here and where we are headed, both now and after death; and *community*, which is the need to find love, acceptance, forgiveness, and a sense of belonging. Here's how the three elements of a healthy life look in a diagram:

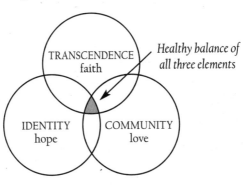

Jesus simply called these three needs; faith, hope and love. The greatest of the three he said is love. All three of these needs are met when we come to God through Jesus Christ. When you receive God's gift of everlasting life, you rest your faith in a power beyond yourself. Although you cannot see God, you are forever anchored in his love, acceptance and forgiveness. That's transcendence.

Secondly, you now have hope for this life and beyond the grave because you have come to know who you were created to be. You have found meaning and purpose to your life. That's identity.

And thirdly, you have come to experience and understand that God loves you and forgives you. Furthermore he helps you love him, become loving and lovable, and places you in a family of believers of about two billion people.

That's community. We finally belong to someone. Together, finding faith, hope and love; transcendence, identity and community, brings lasting fulfillment and eternal joy.

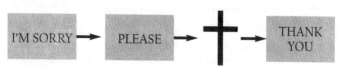

I'm sorry, please and thank you

A friend of mine is an evangelist who travels around
the world telling people how to come to God.
Because he speaks through interpreters to a wide
variety of listeners, he simplifies the process down to
three expressions - I'm sorry, please and thank you.

To say *I'm sorry* means that you realize that you
have sinned against God, you have missed the mark,
you have come short of his divine requirements and
you are sorry for your failure. Another word that the
Bible uses to describe this first step is to repent. To
repent simply means to turn around. You now
understand that you have been walking down the
wrong path and you want to change, so you turn
around and walk in the opposite direction. Rather
than walking away from God, you begin walking
toward him on the right path that he has provided.

The second expression, *please*, is the prayer which
asks God for his forgiveness, and accepts his love
and favour. Sometimes that is easier said than done.
We feel so bad about our past sins that we think
God could never forgive us, or that even if he did
choose to forgive us, we still would not deserve his
love. And it's true; we do not deserve God's love,

acceptance or forgiveness. It is his grace and kindness that he gives to us as a gift which saves us from eternal death. God urges us to simply ask for it and he will freely give his forgiveness to us.

Thirdly comes our grateful response, *thank you.* This word infers that we will now daily purposefully choose to walk in his already prepared pathway with an attitude of humility and gratefulness.

Earlier I suggested a prayer that you might want to say to God. Prayer is simply having a conversation with God, and he has invited us to talk with him any time we choose. He's listening to you right now, fully aware of every thought.

Here is the prayer again:

Father God, I humbly acknowledge that I have sinned and that I am a sinner. I am guilty of deliberate wrongdoing and my sins have separated me from your holy presence. I am helpless in restoring our broken relationship.

I firmly believe that Jesus is your son and that he died on the cross for my sins and suffered in my place, taking the punishment I deserved.

I have thoughtfully counted the cost of following you. I sincerely turn away from my past sins. I willingly surrender to you as my Lord and Master.

I now receive your son, Jesus, as my Saviour. I believe that he has patiently been waiting outside the door of my life knocking. I now open the door. Come in Lord Jesus, and be my Saviour and Friend forever. Amen.

CHAPTER SEVEN

Now What Do We Do?

Just as a young plant, which has been freshly placed in your garden, needs constant care and nourishment, so does your new life in Jesus Christ. Here are four nutrients that I would recommend to sustain you for the rest of your life.

Find a good church

First, find a good church which you can attend and participate in faithfully. Do a survey of three or four in proximity to your home. Ask someone inside the church for a brochure, or if possible set up a meeting with the pastor. Ask if they are a church who believe the Bible is God's word and then see that they relate it in an easy to understand way. You'll get a feel for the health and vitality of the congregation as you walk in on a Sunday morning and as you sit through a worship service. The key is that you should feel encouraged and spiritually stimulated for having been there. Of course, if you are a parent and can take your children to church, you'll want to ensure that there are healthy peers and programs for your children.

Buy a Bible

Secondly, buy a Bible. Bibles come in a variety of translations, from archaic seventeenth century language to modern American colloquialism. They are all good, but you will want one that is easy for you to read and understand. Your local Bible bookstore attendant or your pastor will help you.

1. Look for a good church   2. Buy a Bible
3. Begin talking with God   4. Find a friend

Start reading your new Bible. I'd suggest that you turn to the New Testament (you'll find a table of contents at the front of your Bible) and begin reading from the Gospel of Luke forward. Come back to the rest later. If you read 3 or 4 chapters each day, you will be able to finish the entire Bible in about a year. You can also find many guides and devotional books at a Christian supply store, which will help you understand what you are reading. The "Red Thread Series" written by Barry Buzza are an excellent introduction to what the Bible is all about, as well as how to apply its principles to our everyday lives.

Begin regularly talking and listening to God

Thirdly, begin regularly talking and listening to God. As I mentioned earlier, prayer is simply having a conversation with God - both listening and speaking. You can talk to him either silently or out loud. You can pray in the car, working in your garden or anywhere you are. God is waiting to spend time with you and is always tuned in to your voice. Ask the pastor of your new church to suggest a course or book which will help you learn to pray effectively.

Find a friend

Fourthly, find a friend. Maybe your new church has a class or Bible study group where you can meet somebody with whom you can share your journey. I recommend a church that offers the Alpha Course, which has been designed especially for new believers. Or even better, invite a friend you already know to go with you to church. Just like a log in a fire will grow cold more quickly when it is separated from the bunch, so will we as believers more likely cool off spiritually when we stay away from other believers.

Finally, enjoy the journey! Years before you were even born, God prepared a purpose and a pathway uniquely for you. As you have received his free gift of love, acceptance and forgiveness, you have stepped onto that pathway. You are beginning the most fulfilling, adventuresome and exciting journey that you could have ever imagined! Congratulations!*

In conclusion, my prayer for you is this:

I pray that our loving and kind Father God will continue to lead you on a level and straight path; that he will keep you safe from harm; that he will nourish you in spirit, soul and body; and that he will fill you to overflowing you with his love, peace, joy and courage. Amen.

*The author recommends his first book, *Life Journey*. *Life Journey*, taken from the well-known Twenty-third Psalm - *The Lord Is My Shepherd*, provides for its readers a simple map to your new life of partnership with God. It explains how life works and will answer some of the questions you may have about the meaning and purpose of your life.

TO CONTACT THE AUTHOR:
Email: bbuzza@northsidechurch.ca
Web: www.barrybuzza.com
Surface Mail: 1460 Lansdowne Drive
Coquitlam, BC
Canada
V3E 2N9

OTHER BOOKS BY BARRY BUZZA

Good Mourning

From Darkness to Morning Sunrise in Seasons of Loss
This book describes the process of mourning. Grief is an inner tearing of the soul that we experience in a time of great loss. This book describes the process of good mourning which is necessary to help us walk through a season of grief toward healing. When loss unsettles our life journey and grief rips through our soul, God's intention is that joy will come in our mourning!

Dying Well

Preparing ourselves for the inevitable
The questions this book will answer are:
- How can I prepare myself spiritually for my future death?
- How can I help my family through the loss by taking care of practical issues?
- How can I leave a legacy that will make a difference for years after I'm gone?
- What do you do immediately after someone you love dies?.

The Red Thread
(Books 1, 2 &3)
The life-line which stretches from God to us and back again.

The Red Thread is the story of Jesus, from Genesis to Revelation. It provides a Bible reading guide easy-to-read commentary and practical application for each of the 52 chapters, can be used for individual reading, small group study (a study guide is also available) or for an entire church 1 year Bible overview.

Higher Ground
A Twelve Step Guide to Spiritual Wholeness

This manual is intended as a Twelve Step interactive guide to be used in small group discussion, in conjunction with homework, to guide us through the process of healing the whole person

The Secret of Happiness
I Just Want To Be Happy

The "Secret to Happiness" reveals in a candid and easy to understand way how to find true and lasting happiness.

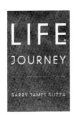

Life Journey
Unveiling the Mystery of Your Life's Destiny
Life Journey addresses our need to anchoring with answers to questions such as: Why do I exist? What is life all about? How can I fill this gaping hole in my soul? Is there a purpose to my life? Do I have a destiny?

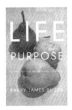

Life Purpose
Why are you here and where are you going?
Through a study of our past, present and dreams of the future, as well as our divinely appointed gifts, talents, skills and passions, Life Purpose promises to help unlock the personal purpose of every reader.

Beta
Basic nutrients for growth in the Christian life
The Alpha course was designed by Nicky Gumbel to help people find a relationship with the God who created them. The Beta course is also an eleven week study to run parallel with Alpha. Beta focuses its participants on the Church and how we can find our place in the body of Christ.